C000103351

Designing Complaint Handling and Service Recovery Strategies

Jochen Wirtz

WS Professional

NEW JERSEY · LONDON · SINGAPORE · BEIJING · SHANGHAI · HONG KONG · TAIPEI · CHENNAI · TOKYO

Published by

WS Professional, an imprint of
World Scientific Publishing Co. Pte. Ltd.
5 Toh Tuck Link, Singapore 596224
USA office: 27 Warren Street, Suite 401-402, Hackensack, NJ 07601
UK office: 57 Shelton Street, Covent Garden, London WC2H 9HE

For orders of individual copies, course adoptions, and bulk purchases: sales@wspc.com
For orders of individual chapters and customized course packs: sales@wspc.com
For adaptations or translation rights and permissions to reprint; rights@wspc.com

Winning in Service Markets Series — Vol. 11
DESIGN COMPLAINT HANDLING AND SERVICE RECOVERY STRATEGIES

ISBN 9781944659417 (pbk)
ISBN 9781944659417 (mobile book)

Desk Editor: Karimah Samsudin

Printed in Singapore

Dedication

To my past and future EMBA and Executive Program participants.

I have been teaching EMBA and Executive Programs for over
20 years. This Winning in Service Markets Series is dedicated to you, the
participants from these programs. You brought so much knowledge and
experience to the classroom, and this series synthesizes this learning for future
EMBA candidates and managers who want to know how to bring their service
organizations to the next level.

Preface

The main objective of this series is to cover the key aspects of services marketing and management, and that is based on sound academic research. Therefore, I used the globally leading text book I co-authored with Professor Christopher Lovelock (Title: *Services Marketing: People, Technology, Strategy*, 8th edition) as a base for this series, and adapted and rewrote it for managers. This is a unique approach.

This series aims to aims to bridge the all-too-frequent gap between cutting edge academic research and theory, and management practice. That is, it provides a strongly managerial perspective, yet is rooted in solid academic research, complemented by memorable frameworks.

In particular, creating and marketing value in today's increasingly service and knowledge-intensive economy requires an understanding of the powerful design and packaging of intangible benefits and products, high-quality service operations and customer information management processes, a pool of motivated and competent front-line employees, building and maintaining a loyal and profitable customer base, and the development and implementation of a coherent service strategy to transform these assets into improved business performance. This series aims to provide the knowledge required to deliver these.

Winning in Service Markets comprises of the following volume:

Vol 1: Understanding Service Consumers
Vol 2: Positioning Services in Competitive Markets
Vol 3: Developing Service Products and Brands
Vol 4: Pricing Services and Revenue Management
Vol 5: Service Marketing Communications
Vol 6: Designing Customer Service Processes
Vol 7: Balancing Capacity and Demand in Service Operations
Vol 8: Crafting the Service Environment
Vol 9: Managing People for Service Advantage
Vol 10: Managing Customer Relationships and Building Loyalty
Vol 11: Designing Complaint Handling and Service Recovery Strategies
Vol 12: Service Quality and Productivity Management
Vol 13: Building A World-Class Service Organization

Contents

Introduction

The first unspoken law of service quality and productivity is: Do it right the first time. However, chances are that the customers may not be always satisfied with some of the services they receive. How well a firm handles complaints and resolves problems frequently determines whether it builds customer loyalty or it should just watch its customers take their business elsewhere. *Design Complaint Handling and Service Recovery Strategies* is the 11th book in the Winning in Service Markets series by services marketing expert Jochen Wirtz to cover the key aspects of services marketing and management based on sound academic evidence and knowledge.

VOLUME 11

Design Complaint Handling and Service Recovery Strategies

A complaint is a gift.

Claus Møller
management consultant and author

Customers don't expect you to be perfect. They do expect you to fix things when they go wrong.

Donald Porter
V.P. British Airways

To err is human; to recover, divine.

Christopher Hart, James Heskett, and Earl Sasser
current and former professors at Harvard Business School
(paraphrasing 18th century poet Alexander Pope)

CUSTOMER COMPLAINING BEHAVIOR

The first unspoken law of service quality and productivity is: Do it right the first time. However, the fact that failures continue to occur cannot be ignored, often for reasons outside of the organization's control such.[1] Many "moments of truth" in service encounters are vulnerable to breakdowns. Distinctive service characteristics such as real-time performance, customer involvement, and people as part of the product can greatly increase the chances of service failures. How well a firm handles complaints and resolves problems frequently determines whether it builds customer loyalty or it should just watch its customers take their business elsewhere (Figure 1).

Customer Response Options to Service Failure

Chances are that the customers may not be always satisfied with some of the services they receive. How do they respond to their dissatisfaction with these services? Do they complain informally to an employee, ask to speak to the manager, or file a formal complaint? Or perhaps just mutter darkly to themselves, grumble to friends and family, and choose an alternative supplier the next time they need a similar type of service?

However, there are few customers who do not complain to the firm about poor service. Research around the globe has shown that most people will choose not to complain, especially if they think it will do no good. Figure 2 depicts the courses of action a customer may take in response to a service failure. This model suggests at least three major steps:

(1) Take some form of *public action* (including complaining to the firm or to a third party, such as customer advocacy groups, consumer affairs or regulatory agencies, or even take the matter to the civil or criminal courts).

(2) Take some form of *private action* (including abandoning the supplier).

(3) Take *no action* (Figure 3).

It is important to remember that a customer can take any one or a combination of actions. Managers need to be aware that the impact of a defection can go far beyond the loss of that customer's future revenue stream. Angry customers often tell other people about their problems,[2]

Figure 1: Organizing framework for managing complaints and service recovery.

Customer Responses to Service Failure
- Take public action (complain to the firm, to a third party, take legal action)
- Take private action (switch provider, spread negative word-of-mouth)
- Take no action

Customer Expectations Once a Complaint Is Made
Customers expect fair treatment along three dimensions:
- Procedural justice: Customers expect a convenient, responsive, and flexible service recovery process
- Interactional justice: The recovery effort must be seen as genuine, honest, and polite
- Outcome justice: The restitution has to reflect the customer loss and inconveniences suffered

Customer Complaining
Why do customers complain?
- Obtain restitution or compensation
- Vent anger
- Help to improve the service
- For altruistic reasons

What proportion of unhappy customers complains?
- 5%–10% complain

Why do unhappy customers not complain?
- It takes time and effort
- The payoff is uncertain
- Complaining can be unpleasant

Who is most likely to complain?
- Higher socioeconomic class customers
- Customers with more product knowledge

Where do customers complain?
- Vast majority of complaints are made at the point of service provision (face-to-face or over the phone)
- Only a small proportion of complaints is sent via email, social media, websites, or letters

Customer Responses to an Effective Service Recovery
- Avoids switching, restores confidence in the firm
- The Service Recovery Paradox: an excellent recovery can even result in higher satisfaction and loyalty than if a service was delivered as promised

Principles of Effective Service Recovery Systems
- Make it easy for customers to provide feedback and reduce customer complaint barriers
- Enable effective service recovery: Make it (1) proactive, (2) planned, (3) trained, and (4) empowered
- Establish appropriate compensation levels: Set based on the (1) positioning of the firm, (2) severity of the service failure, and the (3) importance of the customer. Target for "well-dosed generosity"

Dealing with Complaining Customers:
- Act fast
- Acknowledge customer's feelings
- Do not argue
- Show understanding
- Clarify the facts
- Give customer the benefit of the doubt
- Propose steps to solve the problem
- Keep the customer informed
- Consider compensation
- Persevere to regain customer goodwill
- Improve the service system

Service Guarantees
- Institutionalize professional complaint handling & service recovery
- Drive improvement of processes
- Design: (1) unconditional, (2) easy to understand, (3) meaningful, (4) easy to invoke, (5) easy to collect on, and (6) credible
- Unsuitable for firms with (1) a reputation for excellence, (2) poor quality service, and (3) uncontrollable quality due to external factors (e.g., weather)

Jaycustomers
There are 7 types of jaycustomers:
- The Cheat
- The Thief
- The Rule Breaker
- The Belligerent
- The Family Feuders
- The Vandal
- The Deadbeat

- Jaycustomers cause problems for firms and can spoil the service experience of other customers.
- Firms need to keep track and manage their behavior, including, as a last resort, blacklisting them from using the firm's facilities.

Figure 2: Customer response categories to service failures.

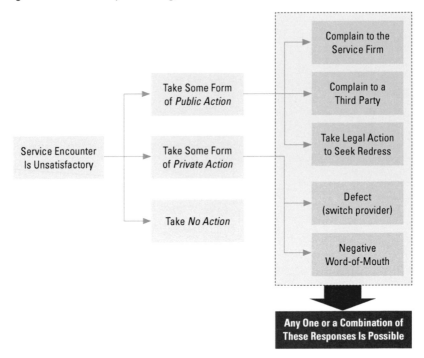

Figure 3: Some customers may just be frustrated but do not take any action to complain, as seen here in an interaction with an online service.

and the Internet allows for unhappy customers to reach thousands of people by posting complaints on bulletin boards, blogs, and even setting up their own websites to talk about their bad experiences with specific organizations.

Understanding Customer Complaining Behavior

To be able to effectively deal with dissatisfied and complaining customers, managers need to understand the key aspects of complaining behavior, starting with the questions posed below.

Why Do Customers Complain? In general, studies of consumer complaining behavior have identified four main purposes for complaining:

(1) *Obtain restitution or compensation.* Consumers often complain to recover some economic loss by seeking a refund, compensation, and/or have the service performed again.[3]

(2) *Vent their anger.* Some customers complain to rebuild self-esteem and/or to release their anger and frustration. When service processes are bureaucratic and unreasonable, or when employees are rude, deliberately intimidating, or apparently uncaring, the customers' self-esteem, self-worth or sense of fairness can be negatively affected. They may become angry and emotional.

(3) *Help to improve the service.* When customers are highly involved with a service (e.g., at a college, an alumni association, or their main banking connection), they give feedback to try and contribute towards service improvements.

(4) *For altruistic reasons.* Some customers are motivated by altruistic reasons. They want to spare other customers from experiencing the same shortcomings, and they may feel bad if they fail to draw attention to a problem that will raise difficulties for others if it remains unnoticed and uncorrected.

What Proportion of Unhappy Customers Complain? Research shows that on average, only 5–10% of customers who have been unhappy with a service actually complain.[4] Sometimes the percentage is far lower. A review of the records of a public bus company showed that formal complaints occurred at the rate of about three complaints for every million passenger trips. Assuming two trips a day, a person would need 1, 370 years (roughly 27 lifetimes) to make a million trips. In other words, the rate of complaints was incredibly low, especially when public bus companies are rarely known for service excellence. Although only a minority of dissatisfied customers complain, there is evidence that consumers across the world are becoming better informed, more self-confident, and more assertive about seeking satisfactory outcomes for their complaints.

Why Do Unhappy Customers Not Complain? A number of studies have identified a number of reasons why customers do not complain. Customers may not want to take the time to write a letter, send an e-mail, fill in a form or make a phone call, particularly if they do not see the service as being important enough to be worth the effort. Many customers see the payoff as uncertain and believe that no one would be concerned about their problem or would be willing to deal with it, and that complaining is simply not worth their while. In some situations, people simply do not know where to go or what to do. Also, many people feel that complaining is unpleasant and may be afraid of confrontation, especially if the complaint involves someone whom the customer knows and may have to deal with again.[5]

Finally, complaining behavior can be influenced by role perceptions and social norms. Customers are less likely to voice complaints in service situations in which they perceive they have "low power" (the ability to influence or control the transaction).[6] This is particularly true when the problem involves professional service providers such as doctors, lawyers or architects. Social norms tend to discourage customer criticism of such individuals.

Who Is Most Likely to Complain? Research findings consistently show that people in higher socio-economic levels are more likely to complain than those in the lower levels. They are better educated, have higher income, and are more socially involved, and this gives them the confidence, knowledge and motivation to speak up when they encounter problems.[7] Furthermore, those who complain also tend to be more knowledgeable about the product in question.

Where Do Customers Complain? Studies show that the majority of complaints are made at the place where the service was received. One of the authors of this book completed a consulting project developing and implementing a customer feedback system. He found that an amazing

99% of customer feedback was given face-to-face or over the phone to customer service representatives. Less than 1% of all complaints were submitted via firms' websites, social media pages, email, letters, or feedback cards. A survey of airline passengers found that only 3% of respondents who were unhappy with their meal actually complained about it, and they all complained to the flight attendants. None of them complained to the company's headquarters or to a consumer affairs office.[8] Also, customers tend to use interactive channels such as face-to-face, or the telephone when they want a problem to be fixed, but use non-interactive channels to complain (e.g., email or websites) when they mainly want to vent their anger and frustration.[9]

In practice, even when customers do complain, managers often do not hear about the complaints made to frontline employees. Without a formal customer feedback system, only a tiny proportion of the complaints may reach corporate headquarters.[10] If unhappy customers have already used other channels of complaint but their problem is not solved, they are more likely to turn to online public complaining. This is due to "double deviation". The service performance already caused dissatisfaction in the first instance, and the resolution of the problem also failed.[11]

What do Customers Expect Once They Have Made a Complaint?

Whenever a service failure occurs, people expect to be treated fairly. However, research has shown that many customers feel that they have not been treated fairly nor received adequate compensation. When this happens, their reactions tend to be immediate, emotional and enduring. In contrast, outcomes that are perceived as fair have a positive impact on customer satisfaction.[12]

Stephen Tax and Stephen Brown found that as much as 85% of the variation in the satisfaction with a service recovery was determined by three dimensions of fairness (Figure 4):[13]

- *Procedural justice* refers to the policies and rules that any customer has to go through to seek fairness. Customers expect the firm to take responsibility, which is the key to the start of a fair procedure, followed by a convenient and responsive recovery process. That includes flexibility of the system and consideration of customer inputs into the recovery process.

Figure 4: Three dimensions of perceived fairness in service recovery processes.

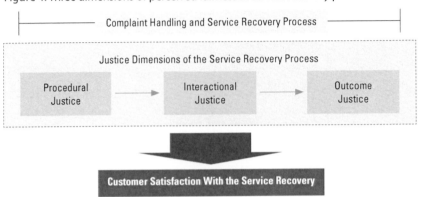

Source: Adapted from Stephen S. Tax and Stephen W. Brown, "Recovering and Learning from Service Failure," *Sloan Management Review* 49, no. 1 (Fall 1998), pp. 75–88.

- *Interactional justice* involves the employees of the firm who provide the service recovery and their behavior toward the customer. It is important to give an explanation for the failure and make an effort to resolve the problem. The recovery effort must also be seen as genuine, honest, and polite.

- *Outcome justice* concerns the restitution or compensation that a customer receives as a result of the losses and inconveniences caused by the service failure. This includes compensation for not only the failure, but also for the time, effort, and energy spent during the process of service recovery.

CUSTOMER RESPONSES TO EFFECTIVE SERVICE RECOVERY

"Thank Heavens for Complainers" was the provocative title of an article about customer complaining behavior, which also featured a successful manager exclaiming, "Thank goodness I've got a dissatisfied customer on the phone! The ones I worry about are the ones I never hear from".[14] Customers who do complain give a firm the chance to correct its problems (including some the firm may not even know of), restore relationships with the complainer, and improve future satisfaction for all.

Service recovery is a term for the systematic efforts of a firm to correct a problem following a service failure and to retain a customer's goodwill. Service-recovery efforts play an important role in achieving (or restoring) customer satisfaction and loyalty.[15] In every organization, things that occur may have a negative impact on relationships with customers. The true test of a firm's commitment to customer satisfaction and service quality is not in the advertising promises, but in the way it responds when things go wrong for the customer. Although complaints tend to have a negative effect on service personnel's commitment to customer service, employees with a positive attitude toward service and their own jobs are more likely to explore additional ways in which they can help customers and view complaints as a potential source of improvement.[16]

Effective service recovery requires thoughtful procedures for resolving problems and handling disgruntled customers. It is critical for firms to have effective recovery strategies, as even a single service problem under the following conditions can destroy a customer's confidence in a firm:

- Failure is totally outrageous (e.g., blatant dishonesty on the part of the supplier).
- Problem fits a pattern of failure rather than being an isolated incident.
- Recovery efforts are weak, serving to compound the original problem rather than correct it.[17]

The risk of defection is high, especially when there are variety of competing alternatives available. One study of customer switching behavior in service industries found that close to 60% of all respondents who reported changing suppliers did so because of a service failure; 25% cited failures in the core service, 19% reported an unsatisfactory encounter with an employee, 10% reported an unsatisfactory response to a prior service failure, and 4% described unethical behavior on the part of the provider.[18]

Impact of Effective Service Recovery on Customer Loyalty

When complaints are resolved satisfactorily, there is a much higher chance that the customers involved will remain loyal. In fact, research has shown that complainants who are satisfied with the service-recovery experience are 15 times more likely to recommend a company than dissatisfied complainants.[19] TARP research found that intentions to repurchase different types of products ranged between 9–37% when customers were dissatisfied but did not complain. For a major complaint, the retention rate increased from 9% when dissatisfied customers did not complain to 19% if the customer complained and the company offered a sympathetic ear but was unable to resolve the complaint to the satisfaction of the customer. If the complaint could be resolved to the satisfaction of the customer, the retention rate jumped to 54%. The highest retention rate of 82% was achieved when problems were fixed quickly, typically on the spot![20]

Complaint handling should be seen as a profit center, not a cost center. When a dissatisfied customer defects, the firm loses more than just the value of the next transaction. It may also lose a long-term stream of profits from that customer and from anyone else who is deterred from patronizing that firm as a result of negative comments from an unhappy friend. However, many organizations have yet to buy into the concept that it pays to invest in service recovery designed to protect those long-term profits.[21]

The Service Recovery Paradox

The *service recovery paradox* describes the phenomenon where customers who experience an excellent service recovery after a failure feel even more satisfied than customers who had no problem in the first place.[22] For example, a passenger may arrive at the check-in counter and find there are no seats for him due to overbooking, even though he has a confirmed seat. To recover the service, the passenger is upgraded to a business class seat, at no additional cost. The customer ends up being more satisfied than before the problem had occurred.

The service-recovery paradox may lead to the thinking that it may be good for customers to experience service failure so they can be delighted as a result of an excellent service recovery. However, this approach would be too expensive for the firm. It is also important to note that the service-recovery paradox does not always apply. In fact, research has shown that the service-recovery paradox is far from universal.[23] For example, a study of repeated service failures in a retail banking context showed that the service-recovery paradox held for the first service failure that was recovered to customers' full satisfaction.[24] However, if a second service failure occurred, the paradox disappeared. It seems that customers may forgive a firm once, but become disillusioned if failures recur. The study also showed that customers' expectations were raised after they experienced a very good recovery; thus, excellent recovery becomes the standard they expect for dealing with future failures.

Whether a customer comes out delighted from a service recovery may also depend on the severity and "recoverability" of the failure — no one can replace spoiled wedding photos, a ruined holiday, or eliminate the consequences of a debilitating injury caused by service equipment. In such situations, it is hard to imagine anyone being truly delighted even when the most professional service recovery is conducted. Compare these examples with a lost hotel reservation for which recovery is an upgrade to a better room, or even a suite. When poor service is recovered by delivery of a superior product, the customer is usually delighted and will probably hope for another lost reservation in the future.

The best strategy is to do it right the first time. As Michael Hargrove puts it, "Service recovery is turning a service failure into an opportunity you wish you never had".[25] Unfortunately, empirical evidence shows that some 40–60% of customers reported dissatisfaction with the service-recovery processes they experienced.[26]

PRINCIPLES OF EFFECTIVE SERVICE-RECOVERY SYSTEMS

Recognizing that current customers are a valuable asset base, managers need to develop effective procedures for service recovery following unsatisfactory experiences. Unfortunately, many service recoveries fail and some of the common causes for failure are shown in *Service Insights 1*. The three guiding principles for how to get it right are as follows: (1) make it easy for customers to give feedback, (2) enable effective service recovery, and (3) establish appropriate compensation levels. A fourth principle, learning from customer feedback and driving service improvements, is discussed in Volume 12 in the context of customer feedback systems. The components of an effective service-recovery system are shown in Figure 5.[27]

SERVICE INSIGHTS 1
Common Service Recovery Mistakes

Here are some typical service recovery mistakes made by many organizations:

- *Managers disregard evidence that shows that service recovery provides a significant financial return.* In recent years, many organizations have focused on cost cutting, paying only lip service to retain their most profitable customers. On top of that, they have also lost sight of the need to respect all their customers.

- *Companies do not invest enough in actions that would prevent service issues.* Ideally, service planners address potential problems before they become customer problems. Although preventive measures do not eliminate the need for good service recovery systems, they greatly reduce the burden on frontline staff and the service recovery system in its entirety.

- *Customer service employees fail to display good attitudes.* The three most important things in service recovery are attitude, attitude and attitude. No matter how well-designed and well-planned the service recovery system is, it would not work well without the friendly and proverbial smile-in-the-voice attitude from frontline staff.

- *Organizations fail to make it easy for customers to complain or give feedback.* Although some improvement can be seen, such as hotels and restaurants offering comment cards and links on their websites and apps, little is done to communicate their simplicity and value to customers. Research shows that a large proportion of customers are unaware of the existence of a proper feedback system that could help them get their problems solved.

Source: Adapted from Rod Stiefbold, "Dissatisfied Customers Requires Service Recovery Plans," *Marketing News* 37, issue 22 (October 27, 2003): 44-45.

Figure 5: Components of an effective service recovery system.

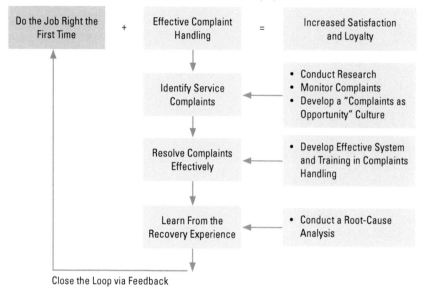

Close the Loop via Feedback

Source: Christopher H. Lovelock, Paul G. Patterson, and Jochen Wirtz, *Services Marketing: An Asia-Pacific and Australian Perspective*, 6th edition (Sydney: Pearson Australia, 2015), p. 419.

Make it Easy for Customers to Give Feedback

How can managers overcome unhappy customers' reluctance to complain about service failures? The best way is to directly address the reasons for their reluctance. Table 1 gives an overview of potential measures that can be taken to overcome these reasons identified earlier. Many companies have improved their complaint-collection procedures by adding special toll-free phone lines, links on their websites and social media pages, and clearly-displayed customer comment cards in their branches. In their customer communications, some companies feature service improvements that were the direct result of customer feedback under the motto "You told us, and we responded".

Enable Effective Service Recovery

Recovering from service failures takes more than just pious expressions of determination to resolve any problems that may occur. It requires commitment, planning, and clear guidelines. Specifically, effective service recovery should be: (1) proactive, (2) planned, (3) trained, and (4) empowered.

Table 1: Strategies to reduce customer complaint barriers.

Complaint Barriers for Dissatisfied Customers	Strategies to Reduce These Barriers
Inconvenience • Difficult to find the right complaint procedure • Effort, for example, writing and mailing a letter	Make feedback easy and convenient: • Put customer service hotline numbers, email the website and/or postal addresses on all customer communications materials (letters, bills, brochures, website, phone book, yellow pages listings, etc.)
Doubtful payoff • Uncertain whether any or what action will be taken by the firm to address the issue the customer is unhappy with	Reassure customers that their feedback will be taken seriously and will pay off: • Have service recovery procedures in place and communicate this to customers, for example, in customer newsletter and website • Feature service improvements that resulted from customer feedback
Unpleasantness • Fear of being treated rudely • Fear of being hassled • Feeling embarrassed	Make providing feedback a positive experience: • Thank customers for their feedback (can be done publicly and in general by addressing the entire customer base) • Train service employees not to hassle and to make customers feel comfortable • Allow for anonymous feedback

Service Recovery Should Be Proactive. Service recovery is ideally initiated on the spot, preferably before customers have a chance to complain (*Service Insights 1*). Service personnel should be sensitive to signs of dissatisfaction, and ask whether customers might be experiencing a problem. For example, the waiter may ask a guest who has only eaten half of his dinner: "Is everything all right, sir?" The guest may say, "Yes, thank you, I am not very hungry", or "The steak is well done but I had asked for medium rare". The second response then gives the waiter a chance to recover the service, rather than have an unhappy diner leave the restaurant and potentially not return.

Recovery Procedures Need to Be Planned. Contingency plans have to be developed for service failures, especially for those that occur regularly and cannot be designed out of the system.[28] For example, revenue management practices in the travel and hospitality industries often result in overbooking, and travelers are denied boarding or hotel guests are "walked" even though they had confirmed seats or reservations. To simplify the task of frontline staff, firms should identify the most common service problems such as overbooking, and then develop solution sets for employees to follow. In contact centers, the customer service representatives have prepared scripts to guide them in a service recovery situation.

Recovery Skills Must Be Taught.[29] As a customer, you may quickly feel insecure at the point of service failure because things are not turning out as expected; so you look to an employee for assistance. However, are they willing and able to help you? Effective training builds confidence and competence among frontline staff, enabling them to turn distress into delight. With effective training of how to handle recovery solution sets for routine service failures (see *Service Insights 2*) and for non-routine service failures, frontline staff can turn distress into delight with confidence and skill.

Recovery Requires Empowered Employees. Service recovery efforts should be flexible and employees should be empowered to use their judgment and communication skills to develop solutions that will satisfy complaining customers.[30] This is especially true for out-of-the-ordinary failures for which a firm may not have developed and trained solution sets. Employees need to be able to make decisions and spend money in order to resolve service problems promptly and recover customer goodwill. At the Ritz-Carlton and Sheraton hotels, employees are given the freedom to be proactive, rather than reactive. They take ownership of the situation and help resolve customers' problems to the best of their ability. In this day and age where online public complaining is gaining popularity, employees may even be empowered to respond online; for example, to complaints in the form of tweets, by tweeting back with a solution to resolve the problem.[31]

SERVICE INSIGHTS 2
Effective Service Recovery in Action

The lobby is deserted. It is not hard to overhear the conversation between the front desk receptionist at the Marriott Long Wharf Hotel in Boston and the late-arriving guest.

"Yes, Dr. Jones, we've been expecting you. I know you are scheduled to be here for three nights. I'm sorry to tell you, sir, but we are booked solid tonight. A large number of guests we assumed were checking out did not. Where is your meeting tomorrow, sir?"

The doctor told the receptionist where it was.

"That's near the Omni Parker House! That's not very far from here. Let me call them and get you a room for the evening. I'll be right back".

A few minutes later the receptionist returned with the good news.

"They're holding a room for you at the Omni Parker House, sir. And, of course, we'll pick up the tab. I'll forward any phone calls that come here for you. Here's a letter that will explain the situation and expedite your check-in, along with my business card so you can call me directly here at the front desk if you have any problems".

The doctor's mood was moving from exasperation towards calm. However, the receptionist was not finished with the encounter. He reached into the cash drawer. "Here is a $50 bill. That should more than cover your cab fare from here to the Parker House and back again in the morning. We don't have a problem tomorrow night, just tonight. And here's a coupon that will get you complimentary continental breakfast on our concierge level on the fifth floor tomorrow morning... and again, I am so sorry this happened".

As the doctor walks away, the hotel's night manager turns to the receptionist, "Give him about 15 minutes and then call to make sure everything went okay".

A week later when it was still a peak period for hotels in that city, the same guest who had overheard the exchange is in a taxi, *en route* to the same hotel. Along the way, he tells about the great service recovery episode he had witnessed the week before. The two travelers arrive at the hotel and make their way to the front desk, ready to check in.

They are greeted with unexpected news: "I am so sorry gentlemen. I know you were scheduled here for two nights. But we are booked solid tonight. Where is your meeting scheduled tomorrow?"

The would-be guests exchange a rueful glance as they give the receptionist their future plans. "That's near the Méridien. Let me call over there and see if I can get you a room. It won't but take a minute". As the receptionist walks away, the tale teller says, "I'll bet he comes back with a letter and a business card".

Sure enough, the receptionist returns to deliver the solution; it is not a robotic script but all the elements from the previous week's show are on display. What the tale teller thought was pure initiative from front desk receptionist the previous week, he now realizes was a planned, seemingly spontaneous yet predetermined response to a specific category of service problem.

Adapted from: Ron Zemke and Chip R. Bell, *Knock Your Socks Off Service Recovery.* New York: AMACOM, 2000, pp. 59–60.

How Generous Should Compensation be?

Vastly different costs are associated with possible recovery strategies. How much compensation should a firm offer when there has been a service failure, or would an apology be sufficient instead? The following rules of thumb can help managers to answer these questions:

- *What is the positioning of your firm?* If a firm is known for service excellence and charges a premium price for quality, then customers will expect service failures to be rare, so the firm should make a demonstrable effort to recover the few failures that do occur and be prepared to offer something of significant value. However, in a mass market business, customers are likely to accept an apology and rework of the service.

- *How severe was the service failure?* The general guideline is "let the punishment fit the crime". Customers expect little for minor inconveniences (in this case, often a sincere apology will do), but a much more significant compensation if there was major damage in terms of time, effort, annoyance, or anxiety was created by the failure.[32]

- *Who is the affected customer?* Long-term customers and those who spend heavily at a service provider expect more, and it is worth making an effort to save their business. One-time customers tend to be less demanding, and have less economic importance to the firm. Hence, compensation can be less, but should still be fair. There is always the possibility that a first-time user will become a repeat customer if he or she is treated well.

The overall rule of thumb for compensation at service failures should be "well-dosed generosity". Being perceived as stingy adds insult to injury, and the firm will probably be better off apologizing than offering a minimal compensation. Overly-generous compensation is not only expensive, customers may even interpret such a response negatively by raising questions in their minds about the soundness of the business and leading them to become suspicious about the underlying motives. Customers may worry about the implications for the employee as well as for the business. Also, over-generosity does not seem to result in higher repeat purchase rates than simply offering a fair compensation.[33] There is also a risk that a reputation for over-generosity may encourage dishonest customers to actively 'seek' service failures.[34] In fact, what customers really want is often just a satisfactory solution to their service problem rather than bells and whistles![35]

Dealing with Complaining Customers

Both managers and frontline employees must be prepared to deal with distressed customers, including jaycustomers who can become confrontational and behave in unacceptable ways towards service personnel who often are not at fault in any way.

Good interactive skills combined with training and on-the-spot thinking are critical for frontline employees to deal with such situations. *Service Insights 3* provides specific guidelines for effective problem resolution, designed to help calm upset customers and to deliver a resolution that they will see as fair and satisfying.[36]

SERVICE INSIGHTS 3
Guidelines for the Frontline:
How to Handle Complaining Customers
and Recover from a Service Failure

1. *Act fast.* If the complaint is made during service delivery, then time is of the essence to achieve a full recovery. When complaints are made after the fact, many companies have established policies of responding within 24 hours, or sooner. Even when full resolution is likely to take longer, fast acknowledgment remains very important.

2. *Acknowledge the customer's feelings.* Do this either tacitly or explicitly (for example, "I can understand why you're upset"). This action helps to build rapport, the first step in rebuilding a bruised relationship.

3. *Do not argue with customers.* The goal should be to gather facts to reach a mutually acceptable solution, not to win a debate or prove that the customer is wrong. Arguing gets in the way of listening and seldom diffuses anger.

4. *Show that you understand the problem from each customer's point of view.* Seeing situations through the customers' eyes is the only way to understand what they think has gone wrong and why they are upset. Service personnel should avoid jumping to conclusions with their own interpretations.

5. *Clarify the facts and sort out the cause.* A failure may result from inefficiency of service, misunderstanding by customers, or the misbehavior of a third party. If you have done something wrong, apologize immediately in order to win the understanding and trust of the customer. The more the customer can forgive you, the less he or she will expect to be compensated. Do not be defensive; reacting defensively may suggest that the organization has something to hide or is reluctant to fully look into the situation.

6. *Give customers the benefit of the doubt.* Not all customers are truthful and not all complaints are genuine. However,

customers should be treated as though they have a valid complaint until clear evidence proves that it is not true. If a lot of money is at stake (as in insurance claims or potential lawsuits), careful investigation needs to be carried out. If the amount involved is small, it may not be worth haggling over a refund or other compensation. However, it is still a good idea to check the records to see if there is a past history of dubious complaints by the same customer.

7. *Propose the steps needed to solve the problem.* When instant solutions are not immediately available, tell customers how the firm intends to take action to deal with the problem. This also sets expectations about the time involved, so firms should be careful not to overpromise!

8. *Keep customers informed of progress.* Nobody likes being left in the dark. Uncertainty causes people to be anxious and stressed. People tend to be more accepting if they know what's going on and receive periodic progress reports. Therefore, people should be kept informed about what is going on regularly.

9. *Consider compensation.* When customers do not receive the service outcomes they believe they have paid for or have suffered serious inconvenience and/or loss of time and money because the service failed, either a monetary payment or some other compensation in kind (e.g., an upgrade on a flight or a free dessert in a restaurant) is appropriate. This type of recovery strategy may also reduce the risk of legal action by an angry customer. Service guarantees often lay out in advance what such compensation will be, and the firm should ensure that all guarantees are met.

10. *Persevere to regain customer goodwill.* When customers have been disappointed, one of the hardest things to do is to restore their confidence and keep the relationship going. Perseverance may be required to defuse customers' anger and to convince them that actions are being taken to avoid a recurrence of the problem. Truly exceptional recovery efforts can be extremely effective in building loyalty and referrals.

11. *Self-check the service delivery system and improve it.* After the customer has left, you should check to see whether the service failure was caused by accidental mistakes or system defects. Take advantage of every complaint to perfect the whole service system. Even if the complaint is found to be a result of a misunderstanding by customer, this implies that some part of your communication system is ineffective.

SERVICE GUARANTEES

One way for particularly customer-focused firms to institutionalize professional complaint handling and effective service recovery is through offering service guarantees. In fact, a growing number of companies offer customers a service guarantee, promising that if service delivery fails to meet pre-defined standards, the customer will be entitled one or more forms of compensation, such as an easy-to-claim replacement, refund or credit. A well-designed service guarantee not only facilitates effective service recovery, but also institutionalizes learning from service failures and subsequent system improvements.[37]

The Power of Service Guarantees

Service guarantees are powerful tools for both promoting and achieving service quality for the following reasons:[38]

(1) They force firms to focus on what their customers want and expect in each element of the service.

(2) They set clear standards, telling customers and employees alike what the company stands for. Payouts to compensate customers for poor service cause managers to take guarantees seriously as they highlight the financial costs of quality failures.

(3) They require the development of systems for generating meaningful customer feedback and acting on it.

(4) They force service organizations to understand why they fail and encourage them to identify and overcome potential fail points.

Figure 6: Hampton Inn includes its "100% satisfaction guaranteed" in its advertising.

(5) They build "marketing muscle" by reducing the risk of the purchase decision and building long-term loyalty.

From the customer's perspective, the primary function of service guarantees is to lower the perceived risks associated with purchase.[39] The presence of a guarantee may also make it easier for customers to complain and they will more likely do so, because they will anticipate that frontline employees will be prepared to resolve the problem and provide appropriate compensation. Sara Björlin Lidén and Per Skålén found that even when dissatisfied customers were unaware that a service guarantee existed before making their complaint, they were positively impressed to learn that the company has a pre-planned procedure for handling failures and to find that their complaints were taken seriously.[40]

The benefits of service guarantees can be seen clearly in the case of Hampton Inn's "100% Hampton Guarantee" ("If you're not 100% satisfied, you don't pay"; see Figure 6). As a business-building program, Hampton's strategy of offering to refund the cost of the room to a guest who expresses dissatisfaction has attracted new customers and also served as a powerful retention device. People choose to stay at a Hampton Inn because they are confident they will be satisfied. At least as important, the guarantee has become a vital tool to help managers identify new opportunities for quality improvement.

In discussing the impact on staff and managers, the vice president–marketing of Hampton Inn stated, "Designing the guarantee made us understand what made guests satisfied, rather than what *we thought* made them satisfied". It became imperative that everyone from reservationists and frontline employees, to general managers and personnel at corporate headquarters, listen carefully to guests, anticipate their needs to the greatest extent possible, and remedy problems quickly so that guests were satisfied with the solution. Viewing a hotel's function in this customer-centric way had a profound impact on the way the firm conducted business.

The guarantee "turned up the pressure in the hose", as one manager put it, showing where "leaks" existed, and providing the financial incentive to plug them. As a result, the "100% Hampton Guarantee" has had an important impact on product consistency and service delivery across the Hampton Inn chain, and it showed a dramatically positive effect on its financial performance. [41]

How to Design Service Guarantees

Some guarantees are simple and unconditional. Others appear to have been written by lawyers and contain many restrictions. The examples in *Service Insights 4* give an idea about which guarantees instill trust and confidence, and would make a customer like to do business with a firm.

SERVICE INSIGHTS 4
Examples of Service Guarantees
United States Postal Service Express Mail Guarantee

Service Guarantee: Express Mail international mailings are not covered by this service agreement. Military shipments delayed due to customs inspections are also excluded. If the shipment is mailed at a designated USPS Express Mail facility on or before the specified deposit time for overnight delivery to the addressee, delivery to the addressee or agent will be attempted before the applicable guaranteed time. Signature of the addressee's agent, or delivery employee is required upon delivery. If a delivery attempt is not made by the guaranteed time and the mailer files a claim for a refund, the USPS will refund the postage unless the delay was caused by: proper retention for law enforcement purposes; strike or work stoppage; late deposit of shipment; forwarding, return, incorrect address or incorrect ZIP code; delay or cancellation of flights; governmental action beyond the control of the Postal Service or air carriers; war, insurrection or civil disturbance; breakdowns of a substantial portion of the USPS transportation network resulting from events or factors outside the control of the Postal Service or Acts of God.

Source: Printed on back of Express Mail receipt, January 2006. (Note that USPS has dramatically improved its guarantee since.)

L. L. Bean's Guarantee

100% Guaranteed. Our products are guaranteed to give 100% satisfaction in every way. Return anything purchased from us at any time if it proves otherwise. We do not want you to have anything from LL Bean that is not completely satisfactory.

Our guarantee is based on something as simple as a handshake — the deal that you'll be satisfied with a purchase, and if you are not, we'll make it right. We guarantee that we'll hold up our end of the bargain. It's just how we do business. If your purchase isn't completely satisfactory, we're happy to accept your exchange or return at any time.

Source: Printed in all L. L. Bean catalogs and on the company's website, http://global.llbean.com/guarantee.html, accessed 26 August 2016.

MFA Group Inc. (a Professional Recruitment Agency)

We "put our money where our mouth is", in two ways:

1. *Money back*: We offer an unconditional money back guarantee — if at any point during the search process you are unhappy with progress, simply address the fact with us and if you are still not 100% satisfied after that discussion, we will cheerfully and unconditionally, refund every cent you have paid as a retainer. No quibble, no hassle, guaranteed period.

2.   *Twelve-month candidate guarantee*: All candidates placed by us are guaranteed for a full 12 months. If, during this period they leave your firm, for any reason whatsoever, we will conduct an additional search, completely free of charge, until a suitable replacement has been found.

Source: MGA Group's website, *http://www.mfagroup.com/recruiting.htm,* accessed 1 June, 2009.

The Bugs Burger Bug Killer Guarantee
(a Pest Control Company)

- You don't owe us a penny until all the pests on your premises have been eradicated.

- If you're ever dissatisfied with the BBBK's service you will receive a refund for as much as 12 months of service — plus fees for another exterminator of your choice for the next year.

- If a guest spots a pest on your premises, the exterminator will pay for the guest's meal or room, send a letter of apology, and pay for a future meal or stay.

- If your premises are closed down because of the presence of roaches or rodents, BBBK will pay any fines, as well as all lost profit, plus $5000.

Source: Reproduced in Christopher W. Hart, "The Power of Unconditional Service Guarantees." *Harvard Business Review* (July-August 1990).

All three service guarantees — from LL Bean, MFA Group and BBBK — are powerful, unconditional, and instill trust. The other guarantee is weakened by the many conditions attached to it. Hart argues that service guarantees should be designed to meet the following criteria:[42]

(1)   Whatever is promised in the guarantee must be totally *unconditional* and there should not be any element of surprise for the customer.

(2)   *Easy to understand and communicate* to the customer so that he is clearly aware of the benefits that can be gained from the guarantee.

Figure 7: To leave a clear stamp of service quality on customers, the guarantee must be unconditional, meaningful, credible, easily understood, invoked and collectable.

(3) *Meaningful to the customer* in that the guarantee is on something important to the customer and the compensation should be more than adequate to cover the service failure.[43]

(4) It should be *easy* for the customer *to invoke* the guarantee.

(5) If a service failure occurs, the customer should *be able to easily collect* on the guarantee without any problems.

(6) The guarantee should be *credible* and believable (Figure 7).

Is Full Satisfaction the Best You Can Guarantee?

Full satisfaction guarantees have generally been considered the best possible design. However, it has been suggested that the ambiguity associated with such guarantees can lead to the discounting of their perceived value. For example, customers may raise questions such as "What does full satisfaction mean?" or "Can I invoke a guarantee when I am dissatisfied, although the fault does not lie with the service firm?"[44] Attribute-specific guarantees (e.g., guaranteed delivery within 24 hours) are highly specific and therefore do not suffer from ambiguity, although their coverage is not comprehensive and limits their appeal. A hybrid version of the full satisfaction and attribute-specific guarantee, referred to as the "combined guarantee", addresses this issue. It combines the wide scope of a full-satisfaction guarantee with the low uncertainty of attribute-specific performance standards. The combined guarantee has been shown to be superior to the pure full-satisfaction or attribute-specific guarantee

They gave me a refund, no questions asked. These companies can be so stupid they need to be more alert.[53]

I've complained that service was too slow, too quick, too hot, too cold, too bright, too dark, too friendly, too impersonal, too public, too private... it doesn't matter really, as long as you enclose a receipt with your letter, you just get back a standard letter and gift coupon.[54]

Firms cannot easily check whether a customer is faking dissatisfaction or truly is unhappy. At the end of this section, we will discuss how to deal with this type of consumer fraud.

The Thief. The thief jaycustomer has no intention of paying and sets out to steal goods and services (or to pay less than full price by switching price tickets, or contesting bills on baseless grounds). Shoplifting is a major problem in retail stores. What retailers euphemistically call "shrinkage" is estimated to cost them huge sums of money in annual revenues. Many services lend themselves to clever schemes for avoiding payment. For those with technical skills, it is sometimes possible to bypass electricity meters, access telephone lines free of charge, or bypass normal cable TV feeds. Riding free on public transportation, sneaking into movie theaters, or not paying for restaurant meals are also popular, not forgetting the use of fraudulent forms of payment such as using stolen credit cards or checks drawn on accounts without any funds. Finding out how people steal a service is the first step in preventing theft or catching thieves and, where appropriate, prosecuting them. However, managers should try not to alienate honest customers by degrading their service experiences. Provision must also be made for honest but absent-minded customers who forget to pay.

The Rule Breaker. Just as highways need safety regulations (including "Don't Jaywalk"), many service businesses need to establish rules of behavior for customers to guide them safely through the various steps of the service process. Some of these rules are imposed by government agencies for health and safety reasons. The sign found in many restaurants that states "No shirt, no shoes, no service" demonstrates a health-related regulation. Air travel provides one of the best examples of rules designed to ensure safety; there are few other environments outside prison where healthy, mentally competent, adult customers are quite so constrained (albeit for good reason).

In addition to enforcing government regulations, suppliers often impose their own rules to facilitate smooth operations, avoid unreasonable demands on employees, prevent misuse of products and facilities, protect themselves legally, and discourage individual customers from misbehaving. For instance, ski resorts are strict on careless skiers who pose risks to both themselves and others. Collisions can cause serious injury and even death. As such, ski patrol members must be safety-oriented and sometimes take on a policing role. Just as dangerous drivers can lose their licenses, dangerous skiers can lose their lift tickets. For example, at Vail and Beaver Creek in Colorado, ski patrollers once revoked nearly 400 lift tickets in just a single weekend. At Winter Park near Denver, skiers who lose their passes for dangerous behavior may have to attend a 45-minute safety class before they can get their passes back. Ski patrollers at Vermont's Okemo Mountain may issue warnings to reckless skiers by attaching a bright orange sticker to their lift tickets. If pulled over again for inappropriate behavior, such skiers may be escorted off the mountain and banned for a day or more. "We're not trying to be Gestapos on the slopes", says the resort's marketing director, "just trying to educate people".

How should a firm deal with rule breakers? Much depends on which rules have been broken. In the case of legally enforceable ones — theft, bad debts, or trying to take guns on an aircraft — the courses of action need to be laid down explicitly to protect employees and to punish or discourage wrongdoing by customers.

Company rules are a little more ambiguous. Are they really necessary in the first place? If not, the firm should get rid of them. Do they deal with health and safety? If so, educating customers about the rules should reduce the need for taking corrective action. The same is true for rules designed to protect the comfort and enjoyment of all customers. There are also unwritten social norms such as "thou shalt not cut in line", although this is a much stronger cultural expectation in the US or Canada than in many countries, as any visitor to Paris or Hong Kong Disneyland can attest! Other customers can often be relied upon to help service personnel enforce rules that affect everybody else; they may even take the initiative in doing so.

There are risks attached to making lots of rules. The firm may become too inflexible and make it appear bureaucratic and overbearing. Instead of being customer-oriented, employees become like police officers, making sure that customers follow all the rules. However, the fewer the rules, the clearer the important ones can be.

The Belligerent. A type of customer probably seen in a store, at the airport, in a hotel or restaurant — red in the face and shouting angrily, or perhaps icily calm and mouthing insults, threats and obscenities. Things do not always work as they should: machines break down, service is clumsy, customers are ignored, a flight is delayed, an order is delivered incorrectly, staff are unhelpful, or a promise is broken. Perhaps the customer in question is expressing resentment at being told to abide by the rules. Service personnel are often abused, even when they are not to blame. If an employee lacks the power to resolve the problem, the belligerent may become still angrier, even to the point of physical attack. Unfortunately, when angry customers rant at service personnel, the latter sometimes respond in kind, thus escalating the confrontation and reducing the likelihood of resolution.

Drunkenness and drug abuse add extra layers of complication. Organizations that care about their employees go to great efforts to develop skills in dealing with these difficult situations. Training exercises that involve role-playing help employees develop the self-confidence and assertiveness needed to deal with upset, belligerent customers (sometimes referred to as "irates"). Employees also need to learn how to defuse anger, calm anxiety, and comfort distress (particularly when there is good reason for the customer to be upset with the organization's performance).

"We seem to live in an age of rage", declared Stephen Grove, Raymond Fisk, and Joby John, noting a general decline in civility.[55] They suggest that rage behaviors are learned via socialization as appropriate responses to certain situations. Anger and dissatisfaction are qualitatively different emotions. Whereas dissatisfied customers had a feeling of non-fulfillment or "missing out" and wanted to find out who or what was responsible for the event, angry customers were thinking how unfair the situation was, sought to get back at the organization, and wanted to hurt someone.[56] The problem of "Air Rage" has attracted particular attention in recent years due to the risks it poses to innocent people (*Service Insights 5*).[57]

SERVICE INSIGHTS 5

Air Rage: Unruly Passengers Pose a Continuing Problem

Joining the term "road rage" — coined in 1988 to describe angry, aggressive drivers who threaten other road users — is "air rage", describing the behavior of violent, unruly passengers who endanger flight attendants, pilots and other passengers. Incidents of air rage are perpetrated by only a tiny fraction of all airline passengers — reportedly about 5,000 times a year — but each incident in the air may affect the comfort and safety of hundreds of other people.

Although terrorism is an ongoing concern, out-of-control passengers pose a serious threat to safety too. On a flight from Orlando, Florida to London, a drunken passenger smashed a video screen and began ramming a window, telling fellow passengers they were about to "get sucked out and die". The crew strapped him down and the aircraft made an unscheduled landing in Bangor, Maine, where US marshals arrested him. Another unscheduled stop in Bangor involved a drug smuggler flying from Jamaica to the Netherlands. When a balloon filled with cocaine ruptured in his stomach, he went berserk, pounding a bathroom door to pieces and grabbing a female passenger by the throat.

On a flight from London to Spain, a passenger who was already drunk at the time of boarding became angry when a flight attendant told him not to smoke in the lavatory and then refused to serve him another drink. Later, he smashed her over the head with a duty-free vodka bottle before being restrained by other passengers (she required 18 stitches to close the wound). Other dangerous incidents have included throwing hot coffee at flight attendants, head-butting a co-pilot, trying to break into the cockpit, throwing a flight attendant across three rows of seats, and attempting to open an emergency door in flight. On a US domestic flight with a tragic outcome, a violent passenger was restrained and ultimately suffocated by other passengers after he kicked through the cockpit door of an airliner 20 minutes before it was scheduled to land in Salt Lake City.

A growing number of carriers are taking air rage perpetrators to court. Northwest Airlines permanently blacklisted three violent travelers from flying on its aircraft. British Airways gives out "warning cards" to any passenger getting dangerously out of control. Celebrities are not immune to air rage. Rock star Courtney Love blamed her "potty mouth" after being arrested on arrival in London for disruptive behavior on board a flight from Los Angeles. Some airlines carry physical restraints to subdue out-of-control passengers until they can be handed over to airport authorities.

In April 2000, the US Congress increased the civil penalty for air rage from $1,100 to $25,000 in an attempt to discourage passengers from misbehaving. Criminal penalties — a $10,000 fine and up to 20 years in jail — can also be imposed for the most serious incidents. Some airlines have been reluctant to publicize this information for fear of appearing confrontational or intimidating. However, the visible implementation of anti-terrorist security precautions have made it more acceptable to tighten enforcement of procedures designed to control and punish air rage.

What causes air rage? Psychological feelings of a loss of control, or problems with authority figures may be causal factors for angry behavior in many service settings. Researchers suggest that air travel, in particular, has become increasingly stressful as a result of crowding and longer flights; the airlines themselves may have contributed to the problem by squeezing rows of seats more tightly together and failing to explain delays. Findings suggest that risk factors for air travel stress include anxiety and an anger-prone personality; they also show that traveling on unfamiliar routes is more stressful than traveling on a familiar one. Another factor may be restrictions on smoking. However, alcohol abuse underlies a majority of incidents!

Airlines are training their employees to handle violent individuals and to spot problem passengers before they start causing serious problems. Some carriers offer travelers specific suggestions on how to relax during long flights. Some airlines have also considered offering nicotine patches to passengers who are desperate for a smoke but are not allowed to light up. Increased security in the air may be curtailing rage behavior on board flights, but concern continues to grow about passenger rage on the ground. An Australian survey of airport employees found that 96% of airport staff had experienced air rage at work: 31% of agents experienced some form of air rage daily, and 15% of agents reported that they had been physically touched or assaulted by a passenger.

Based on information from multiple sources, including: Daniel Eisenberg, "Acting Up in the Air," *Time*, 21 December 1998; "Air Rage Capital: Bangor Becomes Nation's Flight Problem Drop Point," *The Baltimore Sun*, syndicated article, September, 1999; Melanie Trottman and Chip Cummins, "Passenger's Death Prompts Calls for Improved 'Air Rage' Procedures," *The Wall Street Journal*, 26 September 2000; Blair J. Berkley and Mohammad Ala, "Identifying and Controlling Threatening Airline Passengers, *Cornell Hotel and Restaurant Administration Quarterly* 42 (August-September) 2001: 6-24; www.airsafe.com/issues/rage.htm , accessed 26 August 2016.

What should an employee do when an aggressive customer brushes off attempts to defuse the situation? In a public environment, one priority should be to move the person away from other customers. Sometimes supervisors may have to settle disagreements between customers and staff members; at other times, they need to support the employee's actions. If a customer has physically attacked an employee, then it may be necessary to summon security officers or the police. Some firms try to conceal such events, fearing bad publicity. Others however, feel obliged to make a public stand on behalf of their employees, such as the Body Shop manager who ordered an ill-tempered customer out of the store, telling her: "I won't stand for your rudeness to my staff".

Telephone rudeness poses a different challenge. Service personnel have been known to hang up on angry customers, but that action does not resolve the problem. For instance, bank customers tend to get upset upon learning that checks have been returned because the account is overdrawn (which means they have broken the rules), or that a request for a loan has been denied. One approach for handling customers who continue to shout at a telephone-based employee is for the latter to say firmly: "This conversation isn't getting us anywhere. Why don't I call you back in a few minutes when you've had time to digest the information?" In many cases, taking a break to think (and cool down) is exactly what's needed.

Figure 8: Installing surveillance cameras in public car parks can discourage vandalism.

The Family Feuders. People who get into arguments with members of their own family — or worse, with other customers — make up a subcategory of belligerents we call "family feuders". Employee intervention may calm the situation or actually make it worse. Some situations require detailed analysis and a carefully thought out response. Others, such as customers starting a food fight in an upscale restaurant, require an almost immediate response. Service managers in these situations need to be prepared to think on their feet and act fast.

The Vandal. Soft drinks are poured into bank cash machines; graffiti are scrawled on both interior and exterior surfaces; burn holes from cigarettes scar carpets, tablecloths, and bedcovers; bus seats are slashed and hotel furniture broken; customers' cars are vandalized; glass is smashed and fabrics are torn — the list is endless. Customers do not cause all of the damage, of course. Bored or drunk young people are the source of much exterior vandalism. Disgruntled employees have been known to commit sabotage. Much of the problem does originate with paying customers who choose to misbehave. Alcohol and drugs are sometimes the cause, at other times psychological problems may contribute, and carelessness can play a role. There are also occasions when unhappy customers, feeling mistreated by the service firm, try to take revenge in some way.

The best cure for vandalism is prevention. Improved security discourages some vandals (Figure 8). Good lighting helps, as well as open design of public areas. Companies can choose vandal-resistant surfaces and protective coverings for equipment, and rugged furnishings. Educating customers to use equipment properly (rather than fighting with it) and providing warnings about fragile objects can reduce the likelihood of abuse or careless handling. Finally, there are economic sanctions: security deposits or signed agreements in which customers agree to pay for any damage that they cause.

What should managers do if prevention fails and damage is done? If the perpetrator is caught, they should first clarify whether there are any extenuating circumstances (because accidents do happen). Sanctions for deliberate damage can range from a warning to prosecution. As far as the physical damage itself is concerned, it is best to fix it fast (within any constraints imposed by legal or insurance considerations). The general manager of a bus company had the right idea when he said: "If one of our buses is vandalized, whether it's a broken window, a slashed seat, or graffiti on the ceiling, we take it out of service immediately so nobody sees it. Otherwise you just give the same idea to five other characters who were too dumb to think of it in the first place"!

The Deadbeat. Leaving aside those individuals who never intended to pay in the first place (our term for them is "the thief"), there are many reasons why customers fail to pay for services they have received. They are the ones who delay payment. Once again, preventive action is better than a cure. A growing number of firms insist on pre-payment. Any form of ticket sale is a good example of this. Direct marketing organizations ask for your credit card number as they take your order, as do most hotels when you make a reservation. The next best thing is to present the customer with a bill immediately on completion of service. If the bill is to be sent by mail, the firm should send it fast, while the service is still fresh in the customer's mind.

Not every apparent delinquent is a hopeless deadbeat. Perhaps there is a good reason for the delay and acceptable payment arrangements can be worked out. A key question is whether such a personalized approach can be cost justified, relative to the results obtained by purchasing the services of a collection agency. There may be other considerations too. If the client's problems are only temporary, what is the long-term value of maintaining the relationship? Will it create positive goodwill and word-of-mouth to help the customer work things out? These decisions are judgment calls, but if creating and maintaining long-term relationships is the firm's ultimate goal, they are worth exploring.

Consequences of Dysfunctional Customer Behavior

Dysfunctional customer behavior has consequences for frontline staff, other customers, and the organization itself.[58] Employees who are abused may not only find their mood or temper negatively affected in the short run, but may eventually suffer long-term psychological damage. Their own behavior too may take on negative dimensions, such as taking revenge on abusive customers. Staff morale can be hurt, with implications for both productivity and quality.[59]

The consequences for customers can take both positive and negative forms. Other customers may rally to the support of an employee whom they perceive as having been abused; however, bad behavior can also be contagious, leading a bad situation to escalate as others join in. More broadly, being exposed to negative incidents can spoil the consumption experience for many customers. Companies suffer financially when demotivated employees no longer work as efficiently and effectively as before, or when employees are forced to take medical leave. There may also be direct financial losses from restoring stolen or damaged property, legal costs and paying fraudulent claims.

As suggested in the earlier discussion of air rage, the nature of jaycustomer behavior is likely to be shaped by the characteristics of the service industry in which it occurs. *Service Insights 13.6* reports on a study of jaycustomers in the hospitality industry.

SERVICE INSIGHTS 6
Categorizing Jaycustomers in Hotels, Restaurants, and Bars
To learn more about dysfunctional customer behavior in the hospitality industry, Lloyd Harris and Kate Reynolds developed a research project to identify and categorize different types of misconduct. Open-ended interviews, typically lasting one hour (but sometimes longer) were conducted with 31 managers, 46 frontline

employees, and 29 customers. These interviews took place in 19 hotels (all of which had restaurants and bars), 13 restaurants, and 16 bars. A purposive sampling plan was employed, with the goal of selecting informants with extensive participation in and insights of service encounters. All informants had encountered — or had perpetrated — what could be considered as jaycustomer behavior and were invited to give details of specific incidents. In total, the 106 respondents generated 417 critical incidents.

Based on analysis of these incidents, Harris and Reynolds codified eight types of behavior:

1. *Compensation letter writers* who deliberately and fraudulently wrote to centralized customer service departments with largely unjustified complaints in anticipation of receiving a check or gift voucher.

2. *Undesirable customers* whose behavior fell into three subgroups: (a) irritating behavior by "jaykids" and "jayfamilies"; (b) criminal behavior, typically involving drug sales or prostitution; and (c) homeless individuals who used an organization's facilities and stole other customers' refreshments.

3. *Property abusers* who vandalized facilities and stole items, often to keep as souvenirs.

Table 3: Percentage of Respondents Reporting Incidents by Category.

Category	Employees (%)	Customers (%)
Compensation letter writers	30	20
Undesirable customers	39	47
Property abusers	51	20
[Off-duty] service workers	11	11
Vindictive customers	30	22
Oral abusers	92	70
Physical abusers	49	20
Sexual predators	38	0

Source: Lloyd C. Harris and Kate L. Reynolds (2004), "Jaycustomer Behavior: An Exploration of Types and Motives in the Hospitality Industry," *Journal of Services Marketing*, Vol. 18, No. 5, pp. 339–357.

4. *(Off-duty) service workers* who know how to work the system to their own advantage as customers and deliberately disrupt service encounters, either for financial gain or simply to cause problems for frontline staff.

5. *Vindictive customers* who are violent towards people or property, possibly because of some perceived injustice.

6. *Oral abusers* include professional complainers seeking compensation, and "ego hunters" who take pleasure in offending frontline staff and other customers.

7. *Physical abusers* who physically harm frontline staff.

8. *Sexual predators* — often acting in groups — engage in sexual harassment of frontline personnel either verbally or behaviorally.

Some of these behaviors, such as letter writing and property abuse, are covert in nature (that is, not evident to others at the time they are committed). Certain underlying causes assert themselves across multiple categories; they include desire for personal gain, drunkenness, personal psychological problems, and negative group dynamics.

Table 3 shows the percentage of employees and customers reporting incidents within each category. Rather remarkably, with the exception of the "undesirable customers" category, the incidents in the customer column are all self-reports of the respondents' own misbehavior.

The verbatim reports of jaycustomer behavior recorded in this study make for somber, even scary reading. In particular, they demonstrate especially the challenges posed to management and staff by manipulative customers seeking personal financial gain, and by the abusive behavior of individuals, sometimes acting in groups and fueled by alcohol, who appear unconstrained by traditional societal norms.

Source: Lloyd C. Harris and Kate L. Reynolds, "Jaycustomer Behavior: An Exploration of Types and Motives in the Hospitality Industry," *Journal of Services Marketing* 18, No. 5, 2004, 339-357.

Dealing with Customer Fraud

Dishonest customers can take advantage of generous service recovery strategies, service guarantees, or simply a strong customer orientation in a number of ways. For example, they may steal from the firm, refuse to pay for the service, fake dissatisfaction, purposefully cause service failures to occur, or overstate losses at the time of genuine service failures. What steps can a firm take to protect itself against opportunistic customer behaviors?

Treating customers with suspicion is likely to alienate them, especially in situations of service failure. The president of TARP notes:

Our research has found that premeditated rip-offs represent 1–2% of the customer base in most organizations. However, most organizations defend themselves against unscrupulous customers by... treating the 98% of honest customers like crooks to catch the 2% who are crooks.[60]

Using this knowledge, the working assumptions should be, "If in doubt, believe the customer". However, as *Service Insights 7* shows, it's crucial to keep track of customers who repeatedly "experience service failures", and ask for compensation or invoke the firm's service guarantee. For example, one Asian airline found that the same customer lost his suitcase on three consecutive flights. The chances of this truly happening are probably lower than winning in the national lottery, so frontline staff were made aware of this individual. The next time he checked in his suitcase, the check-in staff followed the video image of the suitcase almost from check-in to pick up at the baggage claim carrousel at the traveler's destination. It turned out that a companion collected the suitcase and took it away while the traveler again made his way to the lost baggage counter to report his missing suitcase. This time, the police were waiting for him and his friend.

In another example, Continental Airlines consolidated some 45 separate customer databases into a single data warehouse to improve service and to also detect customer fraud. The airline found one customer who received 20 bereavement fares in 12 months off the same dead grandfather!

To be able to effectively detect consumer fraud, maintaining a central database of all compensation payments, service recoveries, returned goods, and any other benefits given to customers based on special circumstances are needed (i.e., such transactions cannot be retained only at the local or branch level, but must be captured in a centralized system), and it is important to merge customer data across departments and channels for detecting unusual transactions and the systems that allow them.[61]

Research has shown that customers who think they were treated unfairly in any way (refer to our earlier discussion regarding distributive, procedural and interactive fairness) are much more likely to take advantage of a firm's service recovery effort. In addition, consumers tend to take advantage of large firms more often than small ones — customers think that large firms can easily afford the recovery costs. Also, one-time customers are much more likely to cheat than loyal customers, and customers who do not have a personal relationship with service employees are more likely to take advantage of service recovery policies.

Service guarantees are often used as payouts in service recovery, and it has been shown that the amount of a guarantee payout (e.g., whether it is a 10% or 100% money-back guarantee) had no effect on consumer cheating. It seems that customers who cheat for a 100% refund also cheat for 10%, and that customer who does not cheat for 10% also would not do so for 100%. However, repeat purchase intention significantly reduced cheating intent. A further finding was that customers were also reluctant to cheat if the service quality provided was truly high compared to when it was just satisfactory.[62]

These findings suggest a number of important managerial implications:

(1) Firms should ensure that their service recovery procedures are fair.

(2) Large firms should recognize that consumers are more likely to cheat on them and have robust fraud detection systems in place.

(3) Firms can implement and thus reap the bigger marketing benefits of 100% money-back guarantees without worrying that the large payouts would increase cheating by much.

(4) Guarantees can be offered to regular customers or as part of a membership program, because repeat customers are unlikely to cheat on service guarantees.

(5) Truly excellent services firms have less to worry about cheating than the average service provider.

SERVICE INSIGHTS 7
Tracking Down Guests Who Cheat

As part of its guarantee tracking system, Hampton Inn has developed ways to identify guests who appeared to be cheating, using aliases or various dissatisfaction problems to invoke the guarantee repeatedly in order to get the cost of their room refunded. Guests showing high invocation trends receive personalized attention and follow-up from the company's Guest Assistance Team. Wherever possible, senior managers telephone these guests to ask about their recent stays. The conversation might go as follows: "Hello, Mr. Jones. I'm the director of guest assistance at Hampton Inn, and I see that you've had some difficulty with the last four properties you've visited. Since we take our guarantee very seriously, I thought I'd give you a call and find out what the problems were".

The typical response is dead silence! Sometimes the silence is followed by questions of how headquarters could possibly know about their problems. These calls have their humorous moments as well. One individual, who had invoked the guarantee 17 times in what appeared to be a trip that took him across the US and back was asked, "Where do you like to stay when you travel?" "Hampton Inn", came the enthusiastic response. "But", said the executive making the call, "Our records show that the last seventeen times you have stayed at a Hampton Inn, you have invoked the 100% Satisfaction Guarantee". "That's why I like them!" proclaimed the guest (who turned out to be a long-distance truck driver on a per diem for his accommodation expenses).

Source: Christopher W. Hart and Elizabeth Long, *Extraordinary Guarantees* (New York: AMACOM, 1997).

CONCLUSION

Encouraging customer feedback provides an important means of increasing customer satisfaction and retention. It is an opportunity to get into the hearts and minds of the customer. In all but the worst instances, complaining customers are indicating that they want to continue their relationship with the firm, but also that all is not well and they expect the company to make things right. Here, service firms need to develop effective strategies to recover from service failures so that they can maintain customer goodwill. That is vital for the long-term success of the company.

Having professional and generous service recovery systems does not mean "the customer is always right" and that the firm is open to customer abuse. Rather, it is important for the benefit of all (i.e., other customers, service employees, and the service firm) to effectively deal with jaycustomers.

SUMMARY

1. Customer Dissatisfaction

When customers are dissatisfied, they have several alternatives. They can take some form of:

- Public action (e.g., complain to the firm, a third party, or even take legal action).
- Private action (e.g., switch to another provider and/or spread negative word-of-mouth).
- Take no action.

2. Recovering from a Service Failure

To effectively recover from a service failure, firms need to understand customer complaining behavior and motivations and also what customers expect in response.

- Customers typically complain for any combination of the following four reasons; they want:
  - restitution or compensation
  - vent their anger
  - help to improve the service
  - spare other customers from experiencing the same problems (i.e., they complain for altruistic reasons).
- In practice, most dissatisfied customers do not complain as they may not know where to complain, and find it takes too much effort and is unpleasant, and perceive the payoffs of their effort as uncertain.
- The people who are most likely to complain tend to be better educated, have higher income, are more socially involved, and have more product knowledge.
- Customers are most likely to complain at the point of service provision (face-to-face and over the phone). Only a small proportion of complaints is made via other channels such as email, social media, websites, or letters.

ENDNOTES

1   Even failures by other customers also have an impact on how a firm's customers feel about the firm, see Wen-Hsien Huang (2010), "Other-Customer Failure: Effects of Perceived Employee Effort and Compensation on Complainer and Non-Complainer Service Evaluations," *Journal of Service Management*, Vol. 21, No. 2, pp. 191–211.

2   Roger Bougie, Rik Pieters, and Marcel Zeelenberg, "Angry Customers Don't Come Back, They Get Back: The Experience and Behavioral Implications of Anger and Dissatisfaction in Service," *Journal of the Academy of Marketing Science*, 31, No. 4 (2003): 377–393; Florian v. Wangenheim, "Postswitching Negative Word of Mouth," *Journal of Service Research*, 8, No. 1 (2005): 67–78.

3   For research on cognitive and affective drivers of complaining behavior see: Jean-Charles Chebat, Moshe Davidow, and Isabelle Codjovi, "Silent Voices: Why Some Dissatisfied Consumers Fail to Complain," *Journal of Service Research*, 7, No. 4 (2005): 328–342.

4   Stephen S. Tax and Stephen W. Brown "Recovering and Learning from Service Failure", *Sloan Management Review*, 49, No. 1 (Fall 1998): 75–88.

5   A large body of literature has examined consumer complaining behavior. Important studies include: Jean-Charles Chebat, Moshe Davidow and Isabelle Codjovi, "Silent Voices: Why Some Dissatisfied Consumers Fail to Complain," *Journal of Service Research*, 7, No. 4 (2005): 328–342; Nancy Stephens and Kevin P. Gwinner, "Why Don't Some People Complain? A Cognitive-Emotive Process Model of Consumer Complaining Behavior," *Journal of the Academy of Marketing Science*, 26, No. 3 (1998): 172–189; Kelli Bodey and Debra Grace, "Segmenting Service "Complainers" and "Non-Complainers" on the Basis of Consumer Characters," *Journal of Services Marketing*, 20, No. 3 (2006): 178–187.

6   Cathy Goodwin and B.J. Verhage, "Role Perceptions of Services: A Cross-Cultural Comparison with Behavioral Implications," *Journal of Economic Psychology*, 10 (1990): 543–558.

7   Nancy Stephens, "Complaining," in *Handbook of Services Marketing and Management*, Teresa A. Swartz & Dawn Iacobucci (eds.), (California: Thousand Oaks, Sage Publications, 2000), 291; Alex M. Susskind (2015), "Communication Richness: Why some Guest Complaints Go Right to the Top — and Others Don't", *Cornell Hospitality Quarterly*, Vol. 56, No. 3, pp. 320–331.

8   John Goodman, "Basic Facts on Customer Complaint Behavior and the Impact of Service on the Bottom Line," *Competitive Advantage*, June 1999, pp. 1–5.

9   Anna Mattila and Jochen Wirtz, "Consumer Complaining to Firms: The Determinants of Channel Choice," *Journal of Services Marketing*, 18, No. 2 (2004): 147–155; Kaisa Snellman and Tiina Vihtkari, "Customer Complaining Behavior in Technology-based Service Encounters," *International Journal of Service Industry*

Management, 14, No. 2 (2003): 217–231; Terri Shapiro and Jennifer Nieman-Gonder, "Effect of Communication Mode in Justice-Based Service Recovery." *Managing Service Quality*, 16, No. 2 (2006): 124–144.

10   Technical Assistance Research Programs Institute (TARP), *Consumer Complaint Handling in America; An Update Study, Part II* (Washington DC: TARP and US Office of Consumer Affairs, April 1986).

11   Thomas M. Tripp and Yany Gregoire, "When Unhappy Customers Strike Back on the Internet," *MIT Sloan Management Review*, 52, No. 3 (Spring 2011): 37–44; Sven Tuzovic, "Frequent (Flier) Frustration and the Dark Side of Word-of-Web: Exploring Online Dysfunctional Behavior in Online Feedback Forums," *Journal of Services Marketing*, 24, No. 6 (2010): 446–457.

12   Kathleen Seiders and Leonard L. Berry, "Service Fairness: What it is and Why it Matters," *Academy of Management Executive*, 12, No. 2 (1990): 8–20.
      For review on complaint handling and customer satisfaction, see Katja Gelbrich and Holger Roschk, "A Meta-Analysis of Organizational Complaint Handling and Customer Responses," *Journal of Service Research*, 14, No. 1 (2011): 24–43.
      See also Klaus Schoefer and Adamantios Diamantopoulos (2008), "The Role of Emotions in Transaction Perceptions of (In)Justice into Postcomplaint Behavioral Responses," *Journal of Service Research*, Vol. 11, No. 1, pp. 91–103; Yany Grégoire and Robert J. Fisher (2008), "Customer Betrayal and Retaliation: When Your Best Customers Become Your Worst Enemies," *Journal of the Academy of Marketing Science*, Vol. 36, No. 2, pp. 247–261; Zheng Fang, Xueming Luo, and Minghua Jiang (2012), "Quantifying the Dynamic Effects of Service Recovery on Customer Satisfaction: Evidence from Chinese Mobile Phone Markets", *Journal of Service Research*, Vol. 16, No. 3, pp. 341–355; Ana Belén del Río-Lanza, Rodolfo Vázquez-Casielles, Ana María Díaz-Martín (2009), "Satisfaction with Service Recovery: Perceived Justice and Emotional Responses", *Journal of Business Research*, Vol. 62, Vol. 8, pp. 775–781.

13   Stephen S. Tax and Stephen W. Brown "Recovering and Learning from Service Failure", *Sloan Management Review*, 49, No. 1 (Fall 1998): 75–88;
      See also Tor Wallin Andreassen, "Antecedents of Service Recovery," *European Journal of Marketing*, 34, No. 1 and 2 (2000): 156–175; Ko de Ruyter and Martin Wetzel, "Customer Equity Considerations in Service Recovery," *International Journal of Service Industry Management*, 13, No. 1 (2002): 91–108; Janet R. McColl-Kennedy and Beverley A. Sparks, "Application of Fairness Theory to Service Failures and Service Recovery," *Journal of Service Research*, 5, No. 3 (2003): 251–266; Jochen Wirtz and Anna Mattila, "Consumer Responses to Compensation, Speed of Recovery and Apology After a Service Failure," *International Journal of Service Industry Management*, 15, No. 2 (2004): 150–166.
      For a meta-analysis of the effects of fairness on consumer responses, see: Chiara Orsingher, Sara Valentini, and Matteo de Angelis (2010), "A Meta-Analysis of Satisfaction with Complaint Handling in Services", *Journal of the Academy of Marketing Science*, Vol. 38, No. 2, pp. 169–186.

14   Oren Harari, "Thank Heavens for Complainers," *Management Review,* (March 1997): 25–29.

15   Tom DeWitt, Doan T. Nguyen, and Roger Marshall, "Exploring Customer Loyalty Following Service Recovery," *Journal of Service Research,* Vol. 10, No. 3 (2008): 269–281.

16   Simon J. Bell and James A. Luddington, "Coping with Customer Complaints." *Journal of Service Research,* 8, No. 3 (February 2006): 221–233.

17   Leonard L. Berry, *On Great Service: A Framework for Action* (New York: The Free Press, 1995), p. 94.
      For a meta-analysis on the customer attribution process and how to effectively manage customer attributions of service failures see: Yves Van Vaerenbergh, Chiara Orsingher, Iris Vermeir, and Bart Larivière (2014), "A Meta-Analysis of Relationships Linking Service Failure Attributions to Customer Outcomes", *Journal of Service Research,* Vol. 17, No. 4, pp. 381–398.

18   Susan M. Keaveney, "Customer Switching Behavior in Service Industries: An Exploratory Study," *Journal of Marketing,* 59 (April 1995): 71–82.

19   Customer Care Measurement & Consulting (CCMC), *2007 National Customer Rage Study,* Customer Care Alliance, 2007.

20   Technical Assistance Research Programs Institute (TARP), *Consumer Complaint Handling in America; An Update Study, Part II* (Washington DC: TARP and US Office of Consumer Affairs, April 1986). Since this study, CCMC and W. P. Carey School of Business, Arizona State University (ASU) have conducted six follow-on studies, known as the "Customer Rage Studies", to explore important, emerging trends in the customer experience related to complaining behavior and service recovery. For highlights of the latest study, "The 2013 Customer Rage Study", see http://www.customercaremc.com/wp/wp-content/uploads/2014/01/KeyFindingsFrom2013NationalCustomerRageSurvey.pdf.
      Not addressing a service failure or dissatisfaction with a service recovery effort has been shown to result in various negative customer responses, including revenge, rage, and opportunistic behaviors; Yany Grègoire, Daniel Laufer and Thomas M. Tripp (2010), "A Comprehensive Model of Customer Direct and Indirect Revenge: Understanding the Effects of Perceived Greed and Customer Power", *Journal of the Academy of Marketing Science,* Vol. 38, No. 6, pp. 738–758.

21   For a discussion on how to quantify complaint management profitability, see: Bernd Stauss and Andreas Schoeler, "Complaint Management Profitability: What do Complaint Managers Know?" *Managing Service Quality,* 14, No. 2/3 (2004): 147–156).
      For a comprehensive treatment of all aspects of effective complaint management see Bernd Stauss and Wolfgang Seidel, *Complaint Management: The Heart of CRM* (Mason, Ohio: Thomson, 2004); and Janelle Barlow and Claus Møller, *A Complaint is a Gift.* 2nd ed., San Francisco, CA: Berrett-Koehler Publishers, 2008.

22   Celso Augusto de Matos, Jorge Luiz Henrique, and Carlos Alberto Vargas Rossi, "Service Recovery Paradox: A Meta-Analysis," *Journal of Service Research*, Vol. 10, No. 1 (2007): 60–77; Randi Priluck and Vishal Lala, "The Impact of the Recovery Paradox on Retailer-Customer Relationships," *Managing Service Quality*, Vol. 19, No. 1 (2009): 42–59.

23   Stefan Michel and Matthew L. Meuter, "The Service Recovery Paradox: True but Overrated?" *International Journal of Service Industry Management*, Vol. 19, No. 4 (2008): 441–457.

      Other studies also confirmed that the service recovery paradox does not hold universally; Tor Wallin Andreassen, "From Disgust to Delight: Do Customers Hold a Grudge?" *Journal of Service Research*, 4, No. 1 (2001): 39–49; Michael A. McCollough, Leonard L. Berry and Manjit S. Yadav, "An Empirical Investigation of Customer Satisfaction after Service Failure and Recovery," *Journal of Service Research*, 3, No. 2 (2000): 121–137; James G. Maxhamm III, "Service Recovery's Influence on Consumer Satisfaction, Positive Word-of-Mouth, and Purchase Intentions," *Journal of Business Research*, 54 (2001): 11–24; Chihyung Ok, Ki-Joon Back and Carol W. Shankin, "Mixed Findings on the Service Recovery Paradox," *The Service Industries Journal*, Vol. 27, No. 5 (2007): 671–686.

24   James G. Maxham III and Richard G. Netemeyer, "A Longitudinal Study of Complaining Customers' Evaluations of Multiple Service Failures and Recovery Efforts," *Journal of Marketing*, 66, No. 4 (2002): 57–72.

25   Michael Hargrove, cited in Ron Kaufman, UP! Your Service (Singapore: Ron Kaufman Plc. Ltd., 2005): 225.

26   Steven S. Tax and Steven W. Brown (1998), "Recovering and Learning from Service Failure", Sloan Management Review, Vol. 40, No. 1, pp. 75–88; Stephen S. Tax, Stephen W. Brown, and Murali Chandrashekaran, "Customer Evaluation of Service Complaint Experiences: Implications for Relationship Marketing," *Journal of Marketing*, 62, No. 2 (Spring 1998): 60–76.

      For a study in the online environment, see: Betsy B. Holloway and Sharon E. Beatty, "Service Failure in Online Retailing: A Recovery Opportunity," *Journal of Service Research*, 6, No. 1 (2003): 92–105.

27   For a discussion on how to quantify complaint management profitability see: Bernd Stauss and Andreas Schoeler, "Complaint Management Profitability: What do Complaint Managers Know?" *Managing Service Quality*, 14, No. 2/3 (2004): 147–156).

      For a comprehensive treatment of all aspects of effective complaint management, see Bernd Stauss and Wolfgang Seidel, *Complaint Management: The Heart of CRM* (Mason, Ohio: Thomson, 2004); and Janelle Barlow and Claus Móller, *A Complaint is a Gift*. 2nd ed., San Francisco, CA: Berrett-Koehler Publishers, 2008.

28   Christian Homburg and Andreas Fürst, "How Organizational Complaint Handling Drives Customer Loyalty: An Analysis of the Mechanistic and the Organic Approach," *Journal of Marketing*, 69, (July 2005): 95–114.

ABOUT THE AUTHOR

 **Jochen Wirtz** is Professor of Marketing and Vice Dean, Graduate Studies, at the National University of Singapore (NUS), and an international fellow of the Service Research Center at Karlstad University, Sweden. Furthermore, he is the founding director of the dual degree UCLA–NUS Executive MBA Program (ranked globally #6 in the Financial Times 2016 EMBA rankings) and international fellow of the Service Research Center at Karlstad University, Sweden, and Academic Scholar at the Cornell Institute for Healthy Futures (CIHF) at Cornell University, USA. Dr. Wirtz holds a PhD in services marketing from the London Business School and has worked in the field of services for over 25 years.

Professor Wirtz's research focuses on service marketing and has been published in over 200 academic articles, book chapters and industry reports. He is an author or co-author of more than 10 books, including *Services Marketing — People, Technology, Strategy* (8th edition) (World Scientific, 2016), co-authored with Professor Lovelock, which has become one of the world's leading services marketing text book that has been translated and adapted for more than 26 countries and regions, and with sales of some 800,000 copies.

In recognition of his excellence in teaching and research, Professor Wirtz has received more than 40 awards, including the prestigious Academy of Marketing Science (AMS) 2012 Outstanding Marketing Teacher Award (the highest recognition of teaching excellence of AMS globally), and the top university-level Outstanding Educator Award at NUS. He was also the winner of the inaugural Outstanding Service Researcher Award 2010, and the Best Practical Implications Award 2009, both by Emerald Group Publications.

Professor Wirtz was a banker and took the banking exam at Chamber of Commerce and Industry in Munich. He has since been an active management consultant, working with international consulting firms including Accenture, Arthur D. Little and KPMG, and major service firms in the areas of strategy, business development and customer feedback systems. He has also been involved in several start-ups including in Accellion (www.accellion.com), Angeloop (https://angeloop.co), TranscribeMe (www.transcribeme.com), and Up! Your Service (www.upyourservice.com).

Originally from Germany, Professor Wirtz spent seven years in London before moving to Asia. Today, he shuttles between Asia, the US and Europe. For further information, see www.JochenWirtz.com.

ACKNOWLEDGMENTS

First, I would like to thank my mentor, friend and co-author Professor Christopher Lovelock. Since first meeting in 1992, he has become a dear friend who has had significant influence on my thinking and development. We have worked together on a variety of projects, including cases, articles, conference papers, and several books. Winning in Service Markets is, in fact, derived from our best-selling textbook, Services Marketing: People, Technology, Strategy, 8th edition. I am eternally grateful to Christopher for his friendship and support.

Although it's impossible to mention everyone who has contributed in some way to this book through their research, their contributions and discussions at the many academic conferences where we have met, as collaborators on various research projects, and as friends who have always been ready to discuss, criticize, and provide feedback and suggestions. I particularly want to express my appreciation to the following: Tor Andreassen, Norwegian School of Management; John Bateson of Cass Business School; Leonard Berry of Texas A&M University; David Bowen of Thunderbird Graduate School of Management; Richard Chase of the University of Southern California; Jayanta Chatterjee of Indian Institute of Technology at Kanpur, India; James Heskett, Earl Sasser and Leonard Schlesinger, all of Harvard Business School; Bo Edvardsson of University of Karlstad; Pierre Eiglier of Université d'Aix-Marseille III; Michael Ehret of Nottingham Trent University; Raymond Fisk of the Texas State University; Christian Grönroos of the Swedish School of Economics in Finland; Miguel Angelo Hemzo, Universidade de São Paulo, Brazil; Irene Ng of University of Warwick; Jay Kandampully of Ohio State University; Ron Kaufman of UP! Your Service; Sheryl Kimes of Cornell University; Tim Keiningham of Rockbridge Associate; Jos Lemmink of Maastricht University; Xiongwen Lu of Fudan University, China; Paul Maglio of University of California, Merced, USA; Anna Mattila of Pennsylvania State University; Ulrich Orth of Kiel University; Chiara Orsingher of University of Bologna; A. "Parsu" Parasuraman of University of Miami; Paul Patterson of the University of New South Wales, Australia; Anat Rafaeli of Technion-Israeli Institute of Technology, Roland Rust of the University of Maryland; Benjamin Schneider formerly of the University of Maryland; Jim Spohrer of IBM; Javier Reynoso of Tec de Monterrey, Mexico; Christopher Tang of UCLA; Rodoula Tsiotsou of University of Macedonia; and Valarie Zeithaml of the University of North Carolina.

Finally, I'd like to thank you, the reader of this book, for your interest in this exciting and fast-evolving field of services management and marketing. If you have any feedback, please contact me via www.JochenWirtz.com. I'd love to hear from you!